Judy McHelen

INTERVIEW HERO

The Ultimate Guide to the Best Interview Techniques,
Discover Useful Tips and Helpful Guidelines
That Can Help You Land Your Perfect Job

Descrierea CIP a Bibliotecii Naţionale a României
Judy McHelen
　　INTERVIEW HERO. The Ultimate Guide to the Best Interview Techniques, Discover Useful Tips and Helpful Guidelines That Can Help You Land Your Perfect Job / Judy McHelen. – Bucharest: Editura My Ebook, 2020
　　ISBN 978-606-983-608-8

Judy McHelen

INTERVIEW HERO

**The Ultimate Guide to the Best Interview Techniques,
Discover Useful Tips and Helpful Guidelines
That Can Help You Land Your Perfect Job**

My Ebook Publishing House
Bucharest, 2020

CONTENTS

Interview Do's and Don'ts

If you want to increase your chances of obtaining the job for which you are applying, you need to know what is acceptable and what is not when you go for an interview. However, they may seem like small things to a job applicant, doing the right things can make the different in your potential for being hired. It is important to know what things may earn you extra points and those that will take away and cost you the opportunity for that job. Although most people are aware of what to do and not do during an interview, those who are looking for their first job – at least their first full-time job – may not be aware of those things.

Things to do before and during an interview
- Find out something about the company
- Have a hard copy of your resume available
- Make sure you have proper clothing for an interview (professional or business casual depending on the company), freshly laundered and pressed or hung to dry to remove wrinkles
- Prepare a list of questions to ask at the interview

- Have a notebook to take notes during the interview
- Be on time for the interview – if there are circumstances beyond your control call the interviewer and give him or her the option to still see you or reschedule the interview
- Leave your cell phone in the car or turn it off during the interview
- Send a Thank You note to the interviewer as soon as possible after the interview. This increases your chances of being hired.

Things not to do before or during the interview

- Do not schedule interviews too close together in case there are additional things you need to do such as testing or meeting with the department manager
- Do not bring your children or anyone else with you to an interview unless they are also applying for a position
- Never smoke during an interview even if you are allowed to do so and if you smoke right before the interview have gum or breath mints for your mouth and spray to remove the smell from your clothing
- Never snack or chew gum. If you use gum or mints to kill the taste of cigarette smoke, finish them before you go in for the interview
- Stay on topic during the interview and avoid personal discussions
- Do not bring drinks into the interview – if the interviewer asks if you would like coffee, tea or water you may then accept.

Choose Your Words Carefully

When you are speaking with someone about a new position, even if it is with the same company for which you are working be careful of your word choices. Many people lose good opportunities because they fail to adhere to strict professional and grammatical correct language during an interview. If you do not use correct grammar any other time, you will need to use it during a job interview. It may seem perfectly fine to use double negatives and slang when you are dealing with friends and co-workers, but if you want to win positive points during an interview, you have to speak as though you are educated.

During an interview never under any circumstances, use slang or curse words. For some that might mean thinking carefully before speaking but it is a very important task if you hope to find a job or move on to another one. What is acceptable at home or even at your work place is not acceptable in the interviewer's office or other interview-meeting place. Your choice of words can make a difference in whether you are chosen for the job for which you applied. If you aren't sure how well your grammar skills are take a little time to brush up on some common word choices before you go to the interview. Although little things such as ending a sentence with a preposition may go unnoticed during an interview, using incorrect verb forms or slang will be highly noticeable.

The topic of your conversation is another area where you need to be very professional during an interview. Even if you know the interviewer as a friend, you should not use the interview to share jokes or events outside of the interview or related events. There is a time to separate personal and business relationships and the job interview is one of them. Choose your topics carefully, make them related to the interview and skillfully choose your words so that you present yourself as a professional rather than someone who is in need of further education. Do not attempt to use big words whose meaning you do not know just to make yourself look more intelligent than you are – if you use a word in the wrong context you will make yourself appear foolish in the eyes of the interviewer and will probably cost you the position for which you are applying.

Choosing the Best interview Option
with Multiple Requests

What do you do when you send out many resumes and get multiple requests for interviews? If you are unemployed it isn't a problem but what happens when you are looking for a career change but only have a limited amount of time available for interviews? How do you choose from among your requests? One of the best things to do is choose those that match closest to what you are seeking. When you have a limited amount of time it's important to choose those interviews that would be the most beneficial to your career.

If you have several possibilities that might be good career choices, you may need to weighty all of the possibilities including speed of the interview in order to make a good selection. Maybe you can consider taking a few hours off from your current position in order to interview for all of those positions that are good career choices. If you restrict yourself to a certain number of interviews, you may have a difficult time finding the position you want. That doesn't mean you should take a lot of time off to interview for a different position. However, you want to be able to schedule your time so that you can fit in all of the interviews what you want to do is choose to interview with those who can best help your career and where you have the highest potential for being hired. Avoid requests for interviews that do not directly promote your choice of a career.

Once you are able to allot the right amount of time to interview for the positions that best meet your career objectives, you need to make sure you follow proper interview protocol to increase your chances for being hired. That means you want to dress appropriately and have a proper discussion at the interview. You also want to make sure you focus your discussion on the position for which you are applying and avoid any personal discussions that are unrelated to the job application. It's essential to remain focused if you wish to make a career change or enter a career as quickly as possible. Choosing the right interview offers will help you do that without interfering with your current working hours or duties. Be selective yet look to the best career choices at the same time in order to diminish your interview time.

Common Interview Mistakes

It is important when you are looking to secure a position especially during tunes when jobs are limited to present yourself in the best possible light. Job seekers continually make several common mistakes that quite often cost them the position for which they are applying. By educating yourself and avoiding these mistakes, you will greatly increase your chances for a successful interview and thus a new job. It is not very difficult but it does require some commitment and understanding of the importance. Once you know what you may be doing wrong you will be able to understand where you have failed in the past.

Improper dress is one of the first things that will cost you a successful interview. You may think it is acceptable to wear jeans and a t-shirt to an interview because you don't own dress clothes. The truth is jeans are not at all acceptable attire for an interview unless your interview takes place at a construction site or in a dirty warehouse and then only if the interviewer tells you prior to the interview that the location will be dirty. There is never an acceptable time to wear shorts to an interview, not even a shorts outfit and that includes Capri's of any length. The only acceptable attire for an interview unless otherwise instructed by the company with which you are interviewing is skirts and blouses, dresses, and dress slacks with coordinating tops for the ladies and dress or casual slacks with dress shirts for the men.

Bringing a cell phone to the interview is something else that will cost you a successful interview. If you cannot leave your phone in the car, at least have the courtesy to turn it off or put it in silent mode. Unless you have a life-threatening emergency with one of your children or family members there is nothing that cannot wait until the interview is complete. Instruct all friends and family to avoid calling you or sending text messages until you are finished with your interview.

During your interview, you should not even have your cell phone in your hand or within your view. You should not use your cell phone during an interview anymore than you should bring children to an interview, another action that will cause a company to cross you off available candidates quickly. If you cannot find a babysitter for an interview, you surely do not have the ambition to work every day.

Conduct Some Research on the Company

If you are interviewing with a company that is unfamiliar to you conduct some research. In most interviews, the interviewer asks what you feel you can contribute to the company, and it is very difficult to answer that question if you do not know anything about it. You can learn a great deal of information by reading their annual report which is usually displayed prominently in the reception area – make a point to arrive in enough time to read through it while you are waiting. The *About Me* page on the company's website is another good place to locate information.

If you do not have access to a computer at home or work, you can go to the library and look up some information on the company for whom you are considering working. Although it may seem unimportant right now, you will present yourself favorably by learning something about the company – it shows you are sincere and ambitious. When there is a decision to be made between you and someone else who has not taken the time to discover information about the company, you will score more points in the final evaluation.

If you learn something about the company, you can get a better idea whether you will be a good fit and whether you really want to work for that company. The problem with interviewing is you do not always get a clear picture of the company, and you do not want to ask questions and admit you have not done any research. The more you know about the company the better able you and the interviewer will be to decide if you are a good fit for the position in question.

Sometimes there isn't time to conduct a great deal of research but you need to gather enough information to show the interviewer you have at least heard of the company and know what they provide in the way or products and services.

It is also important to find out about a company for which you are considering working because they may be involved in causes in which you do not believe. For example, if they support stem cell research and you do not that may not be a company for which you would want to work. If you know these kinds of things before the interview – or at least before the hiring, process is complete – you can avoid choosing a company who has beliefs contrary to yours.

16

Control of the Interview Conversation

One of the problems that some people have is being able to control the conversation during an interview so that it follows toward professional topics. Engaging the interviewer in personal conversation is not going to give you additional points – in fact, it may actually cause you to lose credibility because it will appear as though you are attempting to obtain the job by making friends with the interviewer. Of course, the interviewer is not faultless because many times this happens at the interviewer's end. However, when you continue to indulge in conversation that covers a variety of personal issues it detracts from the purpose of the interview. That is turn will prevent you from capturing the real purpose of the interview, and from being able to follow the questions that are of importance to you and the interviewer.

Sometimes you will find an interviewer who attempts to extract personal information from you by manipulating the

17

conversation away from professionalism. You want to avoid this kind of conversation and remain strictly with the topics that are essential to the performance of the job for which you are applying. It is important to stay on topic so that you don't overrun the interviewer's time and not be able to find out everything you need to know about the position and the company. It is okay to mention that you are married and have children but there is no need to go into details about either topic nor should the interviewer ask. In fact, if the question comes up about childcare all you really need to say is that you have taken care of that issue.

If you compose a list of questions to ask at the interview, you will avoid delving into personal conversation just to have something to say. You will be busy asking the questions and absorbing the interviewer's answers thus maybe even thinking of additional questions at the same time. The key issue of importance is to remain on the topic of the job and the company and not on topics of a personal nature. By keeping the conversation on topic, you can close the interview on time and have answers to all of the questions you brought with you. You will also be able to develop a better feel for the interview and whether you feel comfortable about securing the position instead of walking away with a feeling of not knowing.

Following the Interview Process

Although things will differ between companies, every company has its own interview process. Before you begin interviewing with a company, you should attempt to familiarize yourself with that process. Some companies allow their Human Resources Department to handle the entire hiring process but in most companies Human Resources does nothing more than the initial interview and presents what it considers qualified applicants to the supervisor and/or department manager who make the final decision. Never go into an interview thinking you will be hired on the spot – that was very common in the past but it is very rare today unless it is a small company in desperate need of help.

Before you are hired by a company, you will usually undergo at least two interviews – one at the Human Resources level and one by someone within the department where you will work if you are hired. In some cases, this may happen in the same day. If Human Resources feels you meet the qualifications the department needs, they may escort you to the department or call the department manager to meet with you while you are already there. For this reason, you want to allow plenty of time if you are scheduling more than one interview in one day. Do not assume that you will be finished with an interview in an hour or so because that is not necessarily true. You have to allow for additional time in case you do have the opportunity to interview with the department manager or supervisor.

Depending on the type of job for which you are applying, you may also have to undergo skills testing. For office positions, this may entail a general skills test, typing test and if the position involves accounting or bookkeeping, you may undergo testing for that as well. Most employers will tell you if testing will be part of the interview process but it never hurts to ask so that you can plan your time accordingly. The worst mistake you can make is to assume every interview is going to be an in and out process – always plan for at least two hours not including travel time, so it is best not to plan more than two interviews in one day unless you know with certainty that you will only spend an hour on each interview. Sometimes you will know this when you make the appointment, and you can sometimes tell if you are given specific times from which to choose how long it will take.

How Effective are Group Interviews?

Probably at least a small percentage of those reading this will have attended at least one group interview. The question is how effective are they? After all, there is nothing personal about them – it is the same information, just drawing on the qualifications of each person in the room. What is their purpose and how do most people feel about them? On a whole, they are not likely to be very effective because most people are less likely to open up about their skills and education when they are with a group of people, especially if it appears many people in the group are on a higher level.

The main question here would be to ask why an employer would even consider a group interview in the first place. In most places it results because they have many applicants for the same position and rather than have individual interviews, they put a group together in order to eliminate those who are not right for the position. It saves time for the Human Resources Department who has to select those that meet the requirements of the department. On the other hand, it should be obvious from the resume whether a person meets the minimum requirements, so wouldn't it be better to bring in only those people who meet those minimum requirements? Fortunately, that is what happens in most cases but there are exceptions, which is where group interviews come into play.

Many people become rather timid and shy in this type of situation, so it really fails to serve the purpose for which it is intended. The more personal individual interview is more likely to help achieve the result that is intended rather than that of the group interview. Why would someone want to discuss details of previous employment in front of a group of people he or she doesn't even know? Of course, you do not know the interviewer until you arrive for the interview, but that is one person. Perhaps any companies that utilize these types of interviews to separate those that are qualified from the rest of the applicants should look toward taking more time to review resumes instead of trying to bring together people who don't know each other into a room at the same time. It certainly takes less time to review resumes than to have to take time to try to select the most qualified applicants from a group.

How Much Should You Tell During the Interview

It can be difficult to know what to say during an interview or how much information you should provide. It is very easy to provide more information than is necessary when you are anxious to be hired for a job. Some applicants make the mistake of thinking the more information they provide the better their chances are of being chosen but the truth is sometimes you can provide too much information, which can cast a negative light on you. There is some information that just doesn't need to be provided – you only need to provide information that is pertinent to the position for which you are applying.

How do you know what to reveal? The best rule of thumb is to only answer direct questions and only provide information that is pertinent to the position for which you are applying. If you were terminated from a previous job and the interviewer doesn't ask about it, you are under no obligation to provide that information. In most cases, the interviewer is only going to be interested in experience that relates to the job for which you are applying unless the position in question was your last one. In that case, do not reveal more information than the interviewer asks. With employers today refusing for the most part to provide any information other than the job title and the dates of your employment, the less you say the better. In fact, many companies are utilized third party agencies to provide job verifications, so most companies are not checking references like they used to do.

Many things that people used to reveal at interviews have been stopped under the discrimination law. For instance, employers are no longer allowed to ask your age or marital status during the interview. Of course, once you are hired these things will be important for insurance purposes. Employers are also not allowed to ask about children or childcare arrangements because in the past women with children were often denied employment because of concerns about who was caring for the children of the employee and who would care for them on holidays. Of course, some may still ask but you are under no obligation to discuss your family arrangements unless they are needed for insurance purposes after you are hired. The more information you reveal the more reasons you give a prospective employer to eliminate your name from qualified applicants.

How to Guarantee a Successful Interview

Interviewing for a job can be one of the most difficult tasks to undergo but if you follow some simple suggestions, you will increase your chances for success. When you have a successful interview, you greatly increase your chances of being hired for the position though there is never a guarantee. However, knowing how to guarantee a successful interview is the first step – you surely will not be hired if you are unsuccessful in the interview phase. Many job seekers fail because they either do not know or do not adhere to proper interview etiquette. Knowing what to do and say at an interview can help make your interview more successful.

The way you dress is the biggest challenge to a successful interview, especially for younger job applicants. Unlike those from the older generations, young people are not into the habit of wearing skirts, dresses and suits and thus do not see the need for having them just for a job interview. Their attitude of "this is the 21st century:" do not hold up when it comes to job interviews, especially if the interviewer happens to be from the generation that believes you wear professional clothing to a job interview. In fact, many law offices and investment firms still adhere to professional dress codes and expect the same from job applicants. You will gain more points by overdressing than under dressing. Always wear professional clothing, or at least business casual clothing – never casual clothing – to an interview. If you do not own dress slacks and a nice b louse or shirt, buy one for your interview or borrow an outfit from a friend or relative.

The way you carry yourself in a business atmosphere will have a positive or negative effect on a successful interview. This is especially important when it comes to the way you handle yourself in the presence of the interviewer. One of the most important things to remember is to maintain eye contact with the interviewer. If you are looking around the room, out the window, in your purse and just not paying attention, the interviewer does not know if you focus on him or her or your mind is wandering on other things. If the interviewer thinks your mind is elsewhere, he or she will end the interview and you will lose any opportunity you may have had of securing a position with that company.

How to Make Your Interview a Success

Some people are very good at interviewing techniques while others do not have the least idea what to do to ensure success. Interviewing can be very stressful, especially for those who are out of work, soon to be out of work or just unhappy with their current position. You can ease a great deal of the stress you suffer preceding and during an interview if you know some of the important things to do in order to assure success. That does not mean you will necessarily be the one the company chooses, but you will increase your chances and learn how to conduct yourself to achieve the highest likelihood for success.

Although this is a common misconception with younger job seekers, dress is very important during an interview. For those who have the idea that a prospective employer will have to accept you as you are remember also that employer does not have to hire you. With so many people out of work today you are playing a fool's game if you think an employer is not going

27

to put personal appearance on the top of the list. If you do not wear professional or at least business casual dress any other time, it is essential to wear that style to an interview. Keep in mind that if you know a company adheres to professional or business attire for its employees, you will hurt your chances if you come to an interview wearing business casual clothing.

Showing the prospective employer you know something about the company, will also help increase your chances of being chosen for the position. When you show you have enough interest in the company to take time to learn about its history and products or services, you will gain points in the mind of the interviewer. In addition having someone that already knows something about the company makes it easier during the training process. It is very time consuming to have to explain to someone who knows nothing about a company why they do certain things or what the purpose is for their existence.

When you focus on the interviewer and what he or she has to say you will also have a better chance for securing the position for which you are interviewing. There is no easier way to lose a potential job than to treat the interviewer as if you are uninterested in what he or she has to say. You attention is of essential importance, so you need to maintain eye contact with your interviewer at all times.

How to Properly Schedule an Interview

When you call to schedule an interview on your own, it is important to remember that there are likely to be others that also want to schedule interviews. Although it is more common for an employer to call applicants in which they are interested, some companies still publish advertisements in the newspaper and ask those who are interested to call to set up an interview. Although you may want to schedule something that is convenient for you, that may not meet with the schedule of the company. If you are interested in securing employment or new employment, you have to be willing to compromise.

When you call to schedule an interview, you have to be willing to take some unpaid time from your current job. Although this may not always be necessary, there are times you may have no other choice. For example, if the company is only interviewing this week, and there is only one slot left, you have to decide how important it is for you to secure an interview for that position. If you do not want your current employer to know you are looking for something else, you may have to think of an excuse or just state you have some personal business to which you must attend rather than lie about why you need the time off. In these cases, you are usually pretty informed about the time – if the schedule runs for an hour, you can be sure your interview will be within that period.

Choose times that are convenient for you and the company and ones that you will not have to change for anything other than an emergency. It is not good interview practice to schedule tentative times for interviews unless it is at the discretion of the interviewer. Sometimes they will make allowances for some who will not show up – maybe because they didn't appear to be really interested and were just going through the motions – so they will fit someone else in tentatively in case that should happen. They may also be unsure of how long an interview will take and will over schedule just to be sure that they can see enough people for the position.

You, on the other hand, must be more firm when you make your interviews and be careful not to allow less time than you actually need.

Informal Interviews Can Help Break the Ice

Although it is not done much at the wage earner level, informal interviews are common in the executive areas. Certainly, there is no reason this should not be a part of the interview process for other employees as well. That doesn't mean anyone has to engage in a breakfast or lunch in order to discuss a new position but there are other informal settings in which one can engage in conversation about a new position. It tends to break the ice, especially for someone who may be coming in from out of town just to interview for the position. There is certainly no protocol that says an interview must be conducted in a stuff office or conference room.

During colder weather, taking a walk along the grounds or sitting in a restaurant for coffee or a cold drink is all that is necessary while during spring and summer an outdoor café may provide a good environment conducive to business conversation. One thing of which you must be careful allowing the informal setting to detract from the purpose of the meeting. You are there to discuss a job opening and have simply chosen to do so informally rather than in the interviewer's office. This type of situation works well for those people who are adverse to formal meetings or in cases where the interviewer may not want someone in the office to know he or she is looking to add additional staff – maybe the new person is there to replace someone who is already there but failing to do a good job.

Informal arrangements can be very helpful for those who have not had an interview in a long time or have just graduated from college and are a little nervous about entering the field of their choice. It's easy enough to provide a relaxing atmosphere in which you can talk without being disturbed by visitors or by telephone calls. These distractions can be not only annoying but add to the stress for your applicant. Any time it's possible you want to make sure your applicant can remain stress free and relaxed so that you are able to easily discuss the issues that are pertinent and keep the conversation directed toward what you can offer this new applicant who is interested in the possibility of choosing your company for his career choice for the long-term.

Interview Attitude Creates Failure or Success

The way you carry yourself and the attitude you project to the interviewer have a great impact on your potential for being hired. There is certainly nothing wrong with attempting to sell yourself to the interviewer but you want to do it by drawing attention to your education and experience and not come across with an attitude that gives the impression you believe your skills are far superior to that of anyone else. Of course that is the image you want to portray – that you are the best person for the job – but you don't want to do it in such a way that it appears you are trying to convince yourself more than selling yourself to the company.

Another part of attitude that should remain concealed is that of your feelings about your current or previous employers. For example, if you were terminated because of something that was not your fault; do not make an issue of it by degrading the company or your supervisor. Since most employers today will not give information other than your job title and the length of your employment, you can downplay the situation immensely. That does not mean you lie about what happened but just do not dwell on it – make it short and simple.

Under no circumstances should you enter your interviewer's office with any kind of attitude that is the result of something that happened before your interview – fight with your boyfriend, girlfriend or spouse, getting a ticket, or any other personal issues. When you arrive at your interview, you need to leave any personal issues outside the door so that you can present the best side of your personality to the interviewer. The interviewer could care less if you had a fight with your spouse before you left for your interview – all he or she wants is to find out if you are qualified for the position that is open with the company.

Do not become irritated or offended if you find out you will have to take a drug and alcohol test if chosen for the job. Your attitude tells the interviewer a great deal, and if you appear agitated over the possibility of a drug test the message you will send is that you have something to hide and will most likely fail the test. That will cause the interviewer to skip over your application or choose someone else.

Treat In Person Job Searches as Potential Interviews

Although most companies do not do on the spot interviews today, there is always that possibility, especially in the retail sector and with small companies. Don't go out dressed in jeans or shorts with your children tagging along unless your sole purpose is to pick up applications to take home and fill out before returning, and even this is not always a good idea, especially during the day when the store manager is likely to be on site. In addition, you run the risk that one of the employees will recognize you as someone who came in to pick up an application and will relay the information to the manager.

Certainly if you just happen to walk into a store that has a help wanted sign you are not going to make a special trip back to the business to pick up an application, but this is not your ordinary course of action nor is it one that you should do on a consistent basis. However, if you go out with the sole intent to look for employment, dress appropriately and leave the children with a sitter in case the company does on the spot interviews. You do not want to kill your chances of being hired because you failed to plan accordingly. Of course, during the Christmas season it is very common for retail businesses to leave applications in plain sight where job seekers can pick one up, take it home and bring it back later. You do want to be certain when you return with the application you area prepared for the possibility of an on the site interview.

Another thing you do not want to do when you are job searching is take a friend with you unless the friend is providing transportation or also job searching. In the case of a friend providing transportation, there is no need for the friend to go inside with you, so you might want to ask your meet to meet you at a nearby coffee shop or similar establishment. Only those friends also seeking employment should come into the building with you and you should not treat it, as any more than a job search meaning do not make it a point to tell the company you have a friend or relative with you who is also seeking employment. This also falls into the category of too much personal chitchat and should be avoided.

Interviewing with Multiple People

Sometimes a company will choose to have an applicant interview with more than one person at the same time instead of having two separate interviews. It saves time for both Human Resources and the department heads when everyone can come together and ask their own questions of the applicant at the same time. It also saves the applicant from having to return for another interview if they are qualified for the position. It should be easy for Human Resources to review the qualifications of each application and determine which people who best suit the requirements of the department. Having everyone meet at the same time will give each person an opportunity to ask questions without repeating the same ones as is the case when applicants meet individually with each person who is a part of the hiring process.

Are interviews involving more than one interviewer effective? Should the applicant be able to interview with each person individually? Unlike group interviews, the applicant is still alone with the interviewers and simply meeting with all of the people who play a part in the hiring process. For the applicant who is taking time from another job to interview, it saves time when he or she can attend to everything at one time. It also saves time for the company because they do not have to allot time for several people at different times. It is more likely to help the choice of applicants when everyone can meet at once – it will also shorten the length of the selection process because what is normally two is three steps is now reduced to one.

This type of interview is effective for both small companies as well as large corporations though corporations are more likely to use this method of interviewing. Although some applicants may not feel comfortable with it, they must consider the fact they will meet with all of these same people at some point during the interviewing process. Often applicants will actually find this type of setting preferable to meeting with Human Resources, asked to stay longer or come back at another time to meet with the department heads that will be actually making the selection. In the total scheme of things it is much easier to meet with everyone at the same time instead of having to come back or stay longer than you had originally planned.

Keys to a Successful Interview Process

Being successful during the interview process goes beyond simply showing the interviewer you have the right qualifications for the job. In fact, being qualified for the job only guarantees you will be granted an interview – it does not guarantee you will be hired for the job. The key to being hired is selling yourself to the interviewer, and that means you have to go beyond proving the extent of your impeccable skills. Do not be too confidant – the most qualified applicant can lose a potential position because he or she possessed poor interviewing skills.

One of the worst mistakes someone can make is to apply for a job for which they are not qualified and try to convince the interviewer they have the skills to perform the job. Even if you think you are the most trainable person in the world, if a company says they want someone with experience you had better either have the experience or be able to learn it quickly. A few years ago a young woman took a temporary job at a university entering information into Excel. The agency did not ask if she knew Excel but she learned it quickly and finished the job in two weeks instead of the month that had been projected. She was ultimately hired by the university and today is a help desk administrator, but not everyone has the capability to do what she did.

No matter how qualified you may be if you do not project the right personal image you will not be hired. Many young people fail miserably in this area because they do not accept the advice of others concerning proper dress for an interview. It is never acceptable to wear jeans, t-shirts and sneakers to job interviews yet many people, especially teenagers are guilty of doing this very thing. The problem is sometimes that if it is their first job they do not own anything else, but if you want to be hired you need to buy proper clothes for interviews. Although restaurants and many retail outlets may not care, many other businesses will certainly reject your application based on the way you dress when you come to an interview. You want to be dressed in professional or at least business casual attire and arrive on time. If you are going to be late because of circumstances beyond your control, call and let the interviewer know and give him or her the option of still seeing you or rescheduling the interview.

Preparation for the Interview

Even if you are going to interview for another job, there are some things you can do to prepare for the interview. You do not want to go into the interview with the attitude "I just came from another job, take me as I am and like it." If you are looking to make a career change, especially one that will mean an increase in pay and/or benefits, you want to make a good impression on the potential employer. Although you may very well let the interviewer know you will be coming from another job, if the dress code is of a casual nature, ask the interviewer if that would be acceptable or ask what the company's dress code is and make your own decision based on that knowledge.

Even if you have mailed, emailed or faxed a copy of your resume it is a good idea to bring a copy with you. Quite often, an interviewer will begin by asking questions concerning information on your resume, and it is much easier for you to follow along if you have a copy of your resume with you. Do not attempt to remember everything that is on your resume especially if you have a lengthy professional career. Attempts to recall dates and events that are on your resume may make you appear unprofessional and unprepared for the interview. In addition many interviewers want a fresh copy of your resume – they have usually made all kinds of notes on the copy they have and would like a fresh copy to view during the interview.

Choose your clothing the night before the interview so that you have time to launder it and press anything that may be wrinkled. Be careful of the colors you choose – you should never choose bright colors that take attention away from you. Dark and pastel shades are preferred and choose styles that are conservative and not too revealing. Although this applies more to women than men do, it is a point that is worth repeating. You want the interviewer to look at you and not at your cleavage, so even if you are well endowed do not think you can use it to win over the interviewer even a male.

Have a notebook to take notes. Even if you have a list of questions you have prepared, there will be some points you will want to recall for later, especially the interviewer's name so that you can send a "thank you" note.

Prepare Your Own Questions

During an interview it's always good to have some questions of your own ready to ask. Even though the interviewer may go through many topics of the job and company, and maybe even cover all of your questions, showing that you have taken the time to prepare some questions shows you have drive and initiative, both qualities that will help you secure the position you seek. In many cases if you decline to ask any additional questions the interviewer sees you as lacking any real initiative thus you have failed at this initial and most important stage of the hiring process.

The questions you develop should be those that are out of the ordinary, not those that interviewers routinely answer. You can develop a different line of questions if you take the time to research the company before the interview because the information you find will never cover all of the things you may want to know. Pick out events from the company's history and ask questions that will provide the interviewer with a topic on which to expand. Be careful when you choose the questions – you don't want to choose those that will stump the interviewer. Choose less obvious questions but also those that the company is more likely to make sure its employees know.

Although you may choose to ask questions about benefits if the interviewer doesn't cover them, do not ask about salary. Many people want to jump into this one quickly, but it makes the interviewer think the salary is more important than the job and is a good way to lose the job before you are ever hired. If you have a minimum salary requirement you can discuss that when the company makes an offer of employment. You also don't want to go too deeply into holidays and vacation thus making it appear you are more interested in the benefits the job offers rather than the position itself. You can get more specific when a job offer is made, and if you don't like the terms you can negotiate or decline the company's offer.

The questions you want to ask are those directly related to the job and the company – history of the company, how it has evolved over the years, sales records, quality standards and the like. As already stated, avoid topics that are specific to the position for which you are applying other than the actual job description.

Proper Conduct at a Job Interview

If you have been doing a lot of interviewing and haven't received any job offers maybe you should look at the way you are conducting yourself. Perhaps you are failing at the interview stage because of something you are doing wrong or something you are doing that you should not be doing. There are always reasons a person fails at job interviews and though it is not always the fault of the job seeker there are times when the fault does lie directly with the job seeker. In order to determine if the fault is yours, review your behavior and the way you present yourself at interviews to locate the source of the problem.

One of the places where many job seekers lose before they even begin is in their personal appearance and hygiene. Before going to an interview for any job make sure your clothing is freshly laundered, free of wrinkles and fits properly. In addition make certain you brush your teeth and that your breath does not smell due to bad breath from food you have eaten or from

45

cigarette smoke. If you must have a cigarette before you attend a job interview, have some mints or gum for your breath and a spray for your clothing to remove the cigarette odor.

When you report to your job interview, leave your cell phone in the car or turn it off completely. If you have children, ask someone else to take responsibility for them until you are finished with your interview. Leave the phone number of the company for life-threatening emergencies – anything else can wait until you finish. There is no easier way to lose the potential for being hired than to have your cell phone ring or be interrupted by a text message during an interview. The rationale is if you cannot leave your problems behind for the time it takes for an interview, what will you do if they hire you?

Another reason you may fail at an interview is that you provide too much personal information. For instance, there is no reason to discuss your boyfriend or husband unless the interviewer asks a question relating to childcare or transportation that may require a general statement.

Always focus your attention on the interviewer and not on other things in the room, what is in your purse or your cell phone. Remember, the interviewer is very busy and does not have time for idle chitchat and deserves your undivided attention.

The Importance of Scheduling Proper
Interview Time Frames

When you are looking for a job, or a new job, it is easy to over schedule, especially if you have a limited amount of time in which to schedule interviews. The problem you may find with doing that is that you run the risk of cutting yourself short in the interview process, not something that will make you look very good. If you are scheduling more than one interview in the same day, you have to be very careful with your schedule. Do not be afraid to tell the interviewer that you would like to make other appointments and would like to know how much time to allow. Does it sound tacky? It does not when you compare it to allowing an hour for the interview and finding out it will take longer because they would like you to meet the department manager or take some skills testing.

It is essential to make sure you schedule enough time between interviews so that you do not have to reschedule one or more. Unless you know otherwise, it is probably best to schedule no more than two per day – one in the morning and one in the afternoon. That gives you plenty of time to spend with each interview without having to become concerned with being late for the next interview. No matter how badly you need a job you do not want to hurt your chances by scheduling too many interviews too close together. This is especially important if you are interviewing with temporary contractors since quite often you can expect to be there two or three hours, sometimes more.

Do not be afraid to tell the interviewer that you have something scheduled at such and such a time so that you can work around that schedule. Quite often, if the interviewer knows you have other interviews and they really want you, they will make a quick decision. This practice was more common in the past than it is now, but it still happens occasionally. Certainly it will depend how quickly the company needs to hire someone but you want to do everything right in order to make certain you will increase your chances for employment with that company. Making a transition from unemployed or underemployed to a new career depends how well you handle the initial interview – selling yourself to the company is the only way to ensure your success.

The First Impression is the One that Counts

I am sure we have all heard the saying that the first impression is the last one, and this is especially true of job interviews. If you cannot present yourself favorably at first glance, you are not going to have s second chance. For those who think it is acceptable to go to an interview wearing jeans and sweats, you should be aware that you have already lost the job no matter how qualified you may be. You want to use the interview as a way to secure that position and in order to do so you must dress the part – in other words Dress to Impress to coin the title of a book on the subject of dressing for an interview.

Even if you are familiar with the company and know, their dress code is casual or business casual, save that for after you are hired. Though there may be instances where business casual may be acceptable, you should never dress casually for a job interview unless you are told to do so by the company and only in cases where the interview is being held in a factory or warehouse where even business casual may be out of place. When you walk into the interview you want to make the interviewer want to take a second look and create the impression that you will be an asset to the company.

Sometimes there may be allowance such as when you work for a company with a casual dress code and you are going for an interview immediately before or after work. In this circumstance, you want to apprise the interviewer of the situation so that it will not cast you in a negative light when you arrive. Certainly if you are going to or coming from another job you don't want to dress in a different way and cast suspicion, especially if you do not desire for your former employer to know you are seeking another position.

Regardless of the circumstances, it is never acceptable to wear clothing that is torn, dirty, wrinkled or ill fitting to an interview. If you are coming straight from another job and your clothing has become soiled take the time to change into something else even if you have to stop at a public restroom to do so. Remember, you will not have a second chance to make an impression.

The Interview Process from Start to Finish

Before you begin to interview for your first job, you want to understand the interview process. It is unlikely that you will only be subjected to one interview – in all likelihood, before you are hired you will interview at least two times. The first interview will be with Human Resources, and if they determine you meet the requirements of the department you will meet with the department head who is responsible for doing the hiring. Sometimes you will meet with the supervisor and the manager for three interviews. In a smaller company, all of this may be combined into one in order to make a selection quickly. You may have either two interviews while you are there, you may be asked to return or you may have an interview that includes several people at the same time.

The interview process will vary depending upon the size of the company. In some smaller companies there may not be a Human Resources department at all or they may be the ones who do the actual hiring of employees. In other companies you may actually interview with the store or department manager. Making the choice that is best for the company is always the ultimate focus, so the better you are at selling yourself during the interview, the sooner you will be able to find the job you seek.

Testing may be another part of the interview process. You usually know about this when you schedule the interview so you can plan your time accordingly. The type of testing you have to do will depend upon the position for which you are applying. Even if you are right out of college with little to no experience, you may be asked to take a skills test just to assess your level of general knowledge. For an office position this may also include a typing test and testing for knowledge with various office applications. You have to be prepared to undergo all of the necessary prerequisites if you want to be hired by any company.

If the company is seriously considering hiring you, they may require you to undergo drug and alcohol testing as well. This is not something that usually will occur until they decide they would like to hire you, but it is something you must do before they will actually make a firm offer of employment.

Time Allotments Between interviews

It can be difficult to decide how much time to allow between interviews, but it is better to allow too much time than not enough. Do not think that one to two hours plus travel time will allow enough time between interviews because that is not always the case. If you are anxious to schedule as many interviews as possible, you might ask the person with whom you schedule the interview to provide more specific information about interview time. However, that may also create a problem if the interviewer is impressed with you and wants you to undergo testing or meet with the head of the department where you would be working.

In order to avoid potential conflicts you should limit your interviews to two a day – one in the morning and one in the afternoon with a gap of at least four to five hours between them.

Certainly if one is in the early morning and another late afternoon, you can try to set something else up when you finish with the first one or schedule something tentatively. You do not want to over schedule and then sit fidgeting while trying to hope you will be able to make the second interview on time. Not only is this kind of behavior distracting to the interviewer who will be able to sense you are trying to rush, it will also cause you to take your focus off what the interviewer is saying while you attempt to rush things along.

Sometimes interviewers will stay after hours to schedule interviews for those who are coming from another job. In most cases when this happens, you are the last interview of the day and there is not as much of a need to rush. At the same time, you also stand less of a chance of being able to meet with the hiring manager and thus may have to schedule a second interview on a different day. Although that may be inconvenient for you, it is also inconvenient for those who must stay behind in order to accommodate your schedule. Keep in mind that not every company is going to be willing to do this – some companies actually have set times they schedule interviews and you can choose only from those times. Always remember you are not the only person applying for the job, so your schedule is not of utmost importance to the person with whom you will be interviewing.

Topics of Discussion for an Interview

Many job seekers want to try to engage the interview into topics of discussion that have nothing to do with the reason they are there. Several problems may result because of this:

- It prevents the interviewer from using time efficiently
- It gives the impression that the job seeker is trying to build a friendship with the interviewer in order to help him or her obtain the job
- It takes the focus off the interview itself
- It cuts into time the interviewer needs for other applicants

The purpose of your interview is not to find out where the interviewer went for dinner or what she or he did over the weekend. Even if you happen to know the interviewer personally, you do not discuss personal topics during your interview. That does not mean you cannot ask a couple questions or discuss one event that may be common to both of you, but you do not go into a lengthy discussion about anything not related to your job application and resume.

There is only a certain amount of time your interviewer has, and if she or he has another interview after yours, engaging in small talk will take time away from another applicant. Even though you want to be the one to receive the job offer you don't want to do that by taking time away from another applicant. Think how you would feel if someone did that to you and you will understand the importance of allowing your interviewer to remain on schedule. Even if you know you are the last interview of the day, there may be other things that are of importance, and you may cause your interviewer to have to work overtime in order to finish things that must be finished before leaving for the day.

By remaining on topics that are related to the job for which you are applying such as your education and experience you will allow the interview process to remain on track and prevent the potential of cutting someone else's time short – or even worse, cutting yours short because you are running into someone else's time. The interviewer needs to ask questions about your education and experience in order to know if you are a fit for the job, so you want to remain on those topics as much as possible in order to remain within the period the interviewer has set aside for you.

Printed by Libri Plureos GmbH in Hamburg, Germany